D1648487

To:
....

From:
....

Words
to Cheer
Your Heart

DEVOTIONAL

Ellie Claire®
gift & paper expressions

Ellie Claire® Gift & Paper Expressions
Franklin, TN 37067
EllieClaire.com
Ellie Claire is a registered trademark of Worthy Media, Inc.

Words to Cheer Your Heart Devotional
© 2017 by Ellie Claire
Published by Ellie Claire, an imprint of Worthy Publishing Group, a division of
Worthy Media, Inc.

ISBN 9781633261785

Stock or custom editions of Ellie Claire titles may be purchased in bulk for
educational, business, ministry, fundraising, or sales promotional use. For
information, please e-mail info@EllieClaire.com

Contributing Authors: Lucinda Secrest McDowell, Victoria Duerstock, Paula
Moldenhauer, Michelle Medlock Adams, Ramona Richards

Compiled by Jill Jones
Cover and interior design by Melissa Reagan
Illustrations by iStockphoto.com
Typesetting by Bart Dawson

Printed in China

1 2 3 4 5 6 7 8 9 HAHA 22 21 20 19 18 17

Contents

Let the godly rejoice.
Let them be glad in God's presence.
Let them be filled with joy.

PSALM 68:3 NLT

Happiest of Homes

Splendor and majesty are before him;
strength and joy are in his dwelling place.

1 CHRONICLES 16:27 NIV

Imagine the safest, happiest home you've ever experienced. God's dwelling place is a million bazillion times better.

What do you see in His throne room? Angels singing? Gold glistening?

Do you see yourself there? You are.

And guess what? You're not just a welcomed guest, you're family. In fact, you're seated with Jesus at the Father's right hand. You get to hang out in this glorious place because you're adopted by the King of kings. God is not some distant deity. He is your own Daddy, your Abba Father. There's no need to demand an audience with Him. From where you are seated you need only lean a little to the left to whisper into your Father's ear. You're special. You're His child!

You're wanted. Seen. Heard.

This place is amazing! Praise songs resound. Joy bubbles out in laughter. Peace permeates every single molecule. Everyone here is family, the kind of family who loves without fear. And there's no scarcity. All is abundant. Every need—physical, spiritual, or emotional—is met.

Here in God's home you receive new perspective. It's not that the struggles that tug at you are no longer important; it's that they aren't all consuming when you're in His house of joy. You can lay the burdens down and simply absorb the sweet goodness that permeates His dwelling.

Thank You, Father, for throwing wide the doors of Your joy house and welcoming me in. Help me to absorb the strength and joy that permeates Your place, and show me how to take these gifts with me into my everyday world.

Joy is the serious business of heaven.

C. S. LEWIS

God Will Fill You Up

*And the believers were filled with joy
and with the Holy Spirit.*

ACTS 13:52 NLT

This past year I was asked to teach at a women's retreat in northern Kentucky. The conference director said their theme was "Joy in Jesus" and asked that I bring three talks on joy, so I prayed for direction. I had lots of clever ideas for three different joy talks, but none of them felt quite right. I knew I needed to hear from God, so I sought Him.

But, as I prayed, you know what God kept speaking to my heart? That several women would come to the women's retreat with little to no joy in their hearts and be super resistant to a perky speaker encouraging them to have more joy. So, I began my first talk by asking, "How many of you almost didn't come when you learned that I'd be speaking about joy all weekend?"

I expected to see a few hands go up, but I never anticipated that so many hands would ease into the air. It was confirmation I'd heard from God, but it was also evidence that many in attendance were hurting, joy-depleted individuals. Looking around at all the hands in the air, I knew we had our work cut out for us that weekend.

But God met us right where we were, healing hearts and making deposits of supernatural joy into each of us.

He will do the same for you. All you have to do is ask Him to fill you up, and you will experience the kind of joy that is unshakable, everlasting, and bubbling over. So, go ahead—ask.

Father, please fill me up
with Your supernatural joy so that
it bubbles over onto others. Amen.

Pray for your ability to share your joy
with others and be a light in this world.

KATHRYN SHIREY

Never Wasted

All discipline for the moment seems not to be joyful,
but sorrowful; yet to those who have been trained by it,
afterwards it yields the peaceful fruit of righteousness.

HEBREWS 12:11 NASB

"I have been in this wheelchair for fifty years now," Joni Eareckson Tada said on the anniversary of the diving accident that broke her neck and left her a quadriplegic. Some might deem such a wasted life. But they wouldn't know Joni.

In the midst of horrific medical challenges, she continues to share that everything we overcome with God's strength prepares us to face all that is ahead. "Ten words have set the course for my life: *God permits what He hates to accomplish what He loves.*"

Are you grieving a devastating loss or a scary medical diagnosis? Is it almost impossible to imagine living a fruitful life under such severe limitations?

Joni would be the first to say that there are more important things in life than walking and having use of your hands. "It sounds incredible, but I really would rather be in this wheelchair knowing Jesus as I do than be on my feet without Him."

Joni took what she had and spent a lifetime speaking up for those with a variety of disabilities. She urged church people to open wide their doors for inclusivity in worship and service. Thousands around the world, including my own son, have been empowered and encouraged.

A life wasted? Hardly.

Lord, forgive me for complaining
when I face a new challenge in life.
Use it to make me more like You.

*Everything you face in your life and overcome
with God's strength today prepares you for what
will cross your path tomorrow. Wasting nothing,
God will use every hardship, every bruise in your life
to strengthen your faith and train you in godliness.*

JONI EARECKSON TADA

Joy of Community

Bear one another's burdens,
and so fulfill the law of Christ.

GALATIANS 6:2 ESV

As an extreme introvert, I'm discovering that the modern world makes it simpler than ever to indulge my tendency to be a hermit. Between no-cost, overnight shipping of everything from books to produce and restaurants that deliver, I could easily never leave the house. Many of my friends feel the same way, and we often talk about this over social media. There are even ways to worship and do small group Bible studies online.

But recently I visited my home church, and my joy in seeing—and hugging!—old friends overwhelmed me. I moved away only a few months ago, but even in that short time I felt lost without a church family. Worshipping together, sharing our faith, and singing old hymns made me miss that community of believers more than ever.

While it's possible to worship God and feel His presence when we are alone—and we need to spend time alone with the Lord—as believers, we also benefit from being in the physical presence of other Christians. Throughout Scripture, we're instructed to gather together, lift each other up, and bear each other's burdens. Seeing faces lit with joy, feeling reassuring touches, and raising our voices together in song is all part of serving Christ (see Hebrews 10:25).

Spending time alone with God is vital to our spirits. But so is taking joy in spending time with other people who worship Him. The joy of community will refresh your soul.

Lord, we praise You with voices joined in worship. We love You and thank You for showing us how to be together in You. Amen.

He will give his people strength.
He will bless them with peace.

PSALM 29:11 TLB

Lips Full of Praise

*Let those who delight in my righteousness shout for joy
and be glad and say evermore, "Great is the LORD,
who delights in the welfare of his servant!
Then my tongue shall tell of your righteousness
and of your praise all the day long."*

PSALM 35:27–28 ESV

There's just something about a praise song, isn't there? Music can either soothe a tortured soul or drown it in angst and misery. Music has been a part of my life for as long as I can remember, and I trained very hard to be an accomplished pianist and vocalist. My piano practice was therapy for me. Sitting on the piano bench, I worked through musical problems while letting stress of school and friends and class fade away.

But you don't need training to know intrinsically that music affects us. When we are slogging through our morning barely accomplishing tasks, an upbeat song with

God-honoring lyrics can sometimes be all it takes to power us forward and motivate us to finish a chore we were dreading, or take care of our babies.

I can't tell you exactly what it is, whether it's positive endorphins or just the way God designed us, but when His praise is on my lips, I am more likely to have a positive mindset and face the day with hope. If you are struggling, the worst thing you can do is to pick music that doesn't turn your face towards Him. When we realize who our help comes from, we can walk through our days in victory.

Dear Lord, I delight in You and Your righteousness! Thank You for providing for my every need. I will have Your praise on my lips throughout the day!

Music speaks what cannot be expressed,
soothes the mind and gives it rest; heals the heart
and makes it whole, flows from heaven to the soul.

ANONYMOUS

 # Songs of Joy

The whole earth is filled with awe at your wonders;
where morning dawns, where evening fades,
you call forth songs of joy.

PSALM 65:8 NIV

Night black gives way to silver. Golden rays glisten, widening until all is bright. Light washes through tree branches, climbs over fences, and peeks in windows. As morning dawns the music of birdsong fills the air, unbidden praise rising from feathered throats.

Slumbering humans sometimes awaken with their own songs, worship rising from an unguarded spirit. When light slips over those in repose, even the weighted soul can't hold back expression. The heart's melody rises with the sun.

The day progresses. Maybe in struggle or bustle praise is not on the mind. But the fragrance of lilacs or the mist cloaking wooded hills gives pause, and the soul whispers, "Wow, God!" A child's giggle is praise. So are love murmurs of a dear old soul.

Soup bubbling on the stove fills the air with whiffs of gratitude. It's worship too. A nod to the One who feeds body and spirit.

Evening comes and casts her shadows.

Whether at oceanside or mountainside, whether gazing across prairie or peering through skyscrapers, we gasp at the glory of the sun's descent. The bright, warm light fades into hues of pink and peach. A cool breeze teases us as the sky transforms. Purple. Navy. Quiet settles, the black blanket waiting for stars to poke light holes.

Creation sighs in awe.

Creator God, I am captured by Your wonders. From morning until evening my heart takes notice, and I offer praise.

The birds upon the tree tops sing their song;
The angels chant their chorus all day long;
The flowers in the garden blend their hue,
So why shouldn't I, why shouldn't you, praise Him too?

ANONYMOUS

Joy Comes in the Morning

Weeping may last through the night,
but joy comes with the morning.

PSALM 30:5 NLT

I've heard this Scripture quoted many times in my life, but I never really meditated on it until I was going through the loss of my mother. I had been crying for weeks after her death, feeling just as hopeless and depressed a month into the grieving process, when I stumbled upon this Scripture once again. I read it and inwardly rolled my eyes, and I heard the Holy Spirit whisper into my heart, "But God didn't say which morning."

That's right! He didn't specify tomorrow morning; He just said "morning." Somehow, that took away all of the pressure. I no longer felt like I had to get over the loss of my mama by the next morning. I realized as I meditated on that Scripture that God didn't expect me to get up the next morning and burst into songs of joy, but the promise that I would someday get up with a song in my heart once again was enough to get me through until "my morning" came.

Grieving, I've learned, is a very personal process. It may take a week or a month or a year or five years to go through, but the good news is this: joy always comes in the morning. So, if your morning of joy hasn't manifested yet, hang on. It's coming....

God, help me to be patient with myself
as I grieve, and help me to trust You
throughout the process. I know You're a good God,
and I choose hope today.
I know my morning is coming. Amen.

Healing is a process that God walks His children
through step-by-step.... Do not lose your hope!
If you are hurting right now due to a loss in your life,
I want to tell you that a new beginning is in front of you.

JOYCE MEYER

If we are cheerful and contented,
all nature smiles...the flowers are more fragrant,
the birds sing more sweetly, and the sun,
moon, and stars all appear more beautiful,
and seem to rejoice with us.

ORISON SWETT MARDEN

Trusting in the Dark

I will lead the blind by ways they have not known,
along unfamiliar paths I will guide them;
I will turn the darkness into light before them
and make the rough places smooth. These are the things
I will do; I will not forsake them.

Isaiah 42:16 NIV

All around me was total darkness. I couldn't find which way to get out of the long hallway. Suddenly fear began to creep into my soul.

Do you ever find yourself "in the dark" concerning an important matter? Perhaps you don't know which medical treatment to seek. Or you need a new place to live but wonder where to search. You may ask why God doesn't appear to be shining any light on a clear decision.

Have you laid your concerns and requests at the feet of Jesus? Prayer is conversation with your heavenly Father. Anyone can do it at any time. But you have to be honest and intentional in conveying your needs and fears. Then you must listen quietly.

This is the hardest part. Trusting that God has it all under control and will answer in His way, in His time. The interim (between your prayer and His answer) may pose a temptation to give up. To choose the darkness rather than wait for the Light.

Don't do it. Instead, rehearse all the many times He has provided for you.

He is still here. He has not abandoned you, nor will He. When you can't see the next step, hold tightly to His hand.

Lord, just because I can't see You doesn't mean You aren't there. Thanks for holding my hand.

When the train goes through a tunnel and the world gets dark, do you jump out? Of course not. You sit still and trust the engineer to get you through.

CORRIE TEN BOOM

Living in the And

> "I am the Alpha and the Omega—the beginning
> and the end," says the Lord God.
> "I am the one who is, who always was,
> and who is still to come—the Almighty One."
>
> REVELATION 1:8 NLT

God lives in the *and*. He's the beginning *and* the end. Jesus is fully God *and* fully man. He is justice *and* mercy. Grace *and* truth. Completely powerful *and* completely gentle.

Humans are uncomfortable in the *and*. We don't know how to live in the present and the future at the same time. We struggle with knowing we are perfect in Christ while we still experience human failure.

When it comes to trials, the *and* is tricky business. Jesus wept. Paul says rejoice always. David says to pour our complaints before God one minute and the next he says he will continually speak God's praises.

Real-life struggles require time to grieve, but in our need for real emotion it's easy to forget the *and*. When we do, life's struggles are harder to bear.

Thankfully we are children of the God of the *and*. Ours is not all or nothing thinking.

The trial is hard *and* God is good. Money is short *and* we have a warm coat. That relationship is strained *and* this relationship is a blessing. Today there are problems and for eternity there is joy.

It is possible to cry *and* laugh in the same hour.

Rejoicing in the *and* gives unlimited access to the good in life.

Lord, today I rejoice in the and, remembering that there is more to my life than the problems I face. I celebrate each good gift in gratitude to You, the gift-giver.

The world is indeed full of peril, and in it there are many dark places; but still there is much that is fair, and though in all lands love is now mingled with grief, it grows perhaps the greater.

J. R. R. TOLKIEN

Bone-deep Weariness

The man declares, I am weary, O God;
I am weary, O God, and worn out.

PROVERBS 30:1 ESV

Have you ever been so tired you could sleep standing up, with the lights on, in the middle of the freeway? My first experience with sleep deprivation happened nearly twenty years ago now, but is the first time I can remember bone-deep weariness.

Just two weeks after the birth of our first daughter by caesarean section, after being sick with hyperemesis gravidarum for the *entire* pregnancy, I made my first outing. I went to see my husband at work and to let everyone meet our daughter. I sat down in a recliner while she was being passed around and I don't remember anything further. My husband shared with me later, I immediately fell asleep after sitting down. Everyone left me alone to sleep for a while since they felt sorry for me! The funny part is that I was on the showroom floor of a high-end furniture store fast asleep. Thankfully I didn't run any customers off—I don't think.

When we are run down physically, we are also likely to be run down mentally and emotionally. A good night's rest or even a decent nap can make you feel like a new person and give you the mental strength to deal with a newborn, toddlers, or aging family members. What a treasure to be able to go to God with our weariness. He is not surprised by anything, not even our physical limitations. He is the one who gives us strength when we are weak, and the capacity to continue moving forward even when we don't know if we can.

In the midst of my weariness, God,
You know me and care for me.
Thank You for supplying all my needs
with Your bountiful care!

*Have courage for the great sorrows of life and patience
for the small ones; and when you have
laboriously accomplished your daily task,
go to sleep in peace. God is awake.*

VICTOR HUGO

God Will Never Leave You

In this godless world you will continue
to experience difficulties. But take heart!
I've conquered the world.

JOHN 16:33 MSG

While I was visiting Oasis Church in Los Angeles one Sunday, one of the pastors shared his testimony of dealing with adversity in life. Some difficulties, he admitted, were due to his own bad choices while others were simply attacks of the enemy. But no matter the reason, those adversities had driven him to a place of desperation, hopelessness, and pain. Sitting on the edge of his friend's futon, where he had been sleeping since his marriage had fallen apart, this broken man cried out to heaven: "God, I know You said You would never leave me or forsake me, but why would You lead me here, to this place in my life that is filled with so much pain? I just don't understand." In that still, small voice, God clearly answered him. "Son, I didn't lead you here, I followed you, never leaving your side, but now that you're ready to follow Me, I will carry you out."

I love that so much. No matter how we arrived at our place of desperation, hopelessness, and pain, God will carry us out. He is our deliverer! Just as He spoke to that broken pastor, "Son, I didn't lead you to the pain but now I will carry you out," God is saying the same thing to you today. He is more than willing to pick you up and carry you out of your pain. You don't have to get your life together first. You don't have to pass some holiness test. You don't have to suffer any more for what you've done. You just have to follow Him.

Father, I have made mistakes,
but I am truly sorry. I am hurting, Lord,
and I don't want to remain in this pain anymore,
so I am asking You to make that way
of escape for me. Please carry me out,
and lead me into the bright future
that I know that You have for me. Amen.

If God brings you to it, He will bring you through it.

ANONYMOUS

Love's Embrace

The minute I said, "I'm slipping, I'm falling," your love, GOD, took hold and held me fast. When I was upset and beside myself, you calmed me down and cheered me up.

PSALM 94:16–19 MSG

Let's get real. Life ain't always a bowl full of cherries. This world of ours can be crushing. Even when the big stuff goes well, little annoyances set us off. We want an attitude adjustment, but sometimes the suffering is too deep for a quick fix.

The book of Psalms give wisdom for those who suffer. In them real people exhibit real emotion. Anger, fear, grief—it's all there. The psalmist says he pours his complaints before God, telling Him all his troubles.

We must get it out.

But negatives don't exist in Psalms in isolation. While many start with wailing, they end with worship. What happens after the purging and before the praise?

The psalmist enters God's presence, recognizing His sovereignty and absorbing His limitless love.

Problems are not the end of the story. Even when we feel we're drowning in them, the glorious love of God pulls us from the deep. You can't lose His love because you have negative emotions, so don't feel guilty when they come. He doesn't stop loving you when life hurts. Instead He holds you fast. He never lets go. God's love is unfailing and never ending and fuller and more wondrous than anything else. Even in pain we can be surprised by joy when we enter His love and rest in His embrace.

Precious God, I believe You hold me tight
in all of life's circumstances.
Please open my heart to receive Your love.
Calm me down and cheer me up.

Joy is not necessarily the absence of suffering,
it is the presence of God.

SAM STORMS

God and the Hair Dryer

Beloved, I pray that all may go well with you
and that you may be in good health,
as it goes well with your soul.

3 JOHN 1:2 ESV

I never thought I could find God under a hair dryer, but I did. And I needed to.

I'd had one of those weeks when I'd said "Yes!" to far too many projects, too many game practices, and too many errands. Exhausted and grouchy, the quality of my work had faltered, and I'd snapped at one of my best friends over the phone. Later, I prepared to apologize when she called to tell me she'd made a hair appointment for me. I was stunned. "You're exhausted," she explained. "Go take care of yourself."

Instead of pushing on with work and other duties, I listened. My hair reacts badly to being blown dry, so after two hours of being pampered, my stylist put me under a stationary hair dryer. The heat relaxed me, and my mind and spirit felt rejuvenated. I reached out, and in the isolation of that dryer, I began to pray, feeling God's closeness and reassurance.

When we focus on caring and doing for others, we can easily forget ourselves. Yet God never meant for us to work until we were drained of energy and enthusiasm—not even for Him. God cares tenderly for all of us, and we better serve His kingdom when we are at our best.

Lord, guide us as we work for You and our families, and help us remember to seek rest and renewal along the journey. Amen.

Be patient with yourself. Self-growth is tender; it's holy ground. There's no greater investment.

STEPHEN COVEY

A tranquil heart gives life to the flesh.

PROVERBS 14:30 ESV

Divided by Distraction

Martha was distracted with much serving. And she went up to him and said, "Lord, do you not care that my sister has left me to serve alone? Tell her then to help me." But the Lord answered her, "Martha, Martha, you are anxious and troubled about many things, but one thing is necessary."

LUKE 10:40–42 ESV

I've been blessed by my study of this story for many years now. I am such a Martha at my core. Forever busy doing, juggling, drowning in the workload of motherhood, serving at church, working, etc. But I long to be Mary—to let it all go and focus on Him. Maturing in my faith, I am learning to balance my natural tendencies to go and do and be all things to all people, with the importance of learning and knowing Christ and His Word and spending quality time at His feet.

The Greek word *merimnao*, the word the Lord uses in verse 41 when He says "anxious," carries the idea of division or fractured. Martha's focus was fractured when she was in the presence of the Lord. How often when I am in the presence of the Lord during my own worship or devotional time am I really fractured in my approach? My mind flits from place to place with the things of the day, the week, and more, and instead of my focus staying firmly planted on Him, I find myself completely divided. What an excellent reminder for me, especially in seasons of extreme stress and care, to concentrate my focus on Him. To remember the "one thing" in the midst of my myriad thoughts, and to rest in the care He has promised.

Gracious Father, I thank You
for caring to remind me that I am prone
to wander and to distraction.
Thank You for gently and lovingly
pulling me back to focus on the one thing!

*Normal people live distracted, rarely fully present.
Weird people silence the distractions
and remain fully in the moment.*

CRAIG GROESCHEL

As God loveth a cheerful giver,
so He also loveth a cheerful taker,
who takes hold on his gifts
with a glad heart.

JOHN DONNE

Resting Faith

I waited patiently for the LORD to help me,
and he turned to me and heard my cry. He lifted me out
of the pit of despair, out of the mud and the mire.
He set my feet on solid ground and steadied me as I walked
along. He has given me a new song to sing, a hymn of praise
to our God. Many will see what he has done and be amazed.
They will put their trust in the LORD.

PSALM 40:1–3 NLT

We Christians love our tool belts. Is life hard? Just pull out a Bible verse and nail it on top of the pain. Take a Phillips-head and tweak those emotions with a praise song. Grab a saw to cut away negative talk. Focus on a scripted prayer to level out the thinking.

Tools are helpful. Sometimes even necessary. Churches and individuals have their favorite ones.

But there's a time for no determined efforts. No practiced disciplines. No self-improvement. In some situations we feel too weary to put on our tool belt, much less start the remodeling project.

What if that's okay?

Perhaps the deepest faith simply lies down when it is tired, trusting the One who loves to rebuild.

This kind of faith waits on the Lord. It doesn't give up. It gives in to the Spirit's whisper. It reclines in verdant pastures and rests beside calm, quiet waters.

Questions may come. Darkness sometimes descends.

But faith waits upon God, cries out for more faith when more faith is needed.

Faith believes transformation is coming. Faith trusts that the One who is faithful will Himself pull us from the pit and put our feet on solid ground. He will hear our cries and restore our soul.

Lord, I "give in" to faith. To You.
I choose rest over striving.
Transforming grace over tool belt living.

Transformation comes, in the end,
not from an act of will, but an act of grace.
We can only ask for it and keep asking.

PHILIP YANCEY

Is It Time to Just Do Nothing?

*Come with me by yourselves
to a quiet place and get some rest.*

MARK 6:31 NIV

I leaned back into the chaise lounge, fully absorbing my task at hand: doing absolutely nothing. Not reading. Not writing. Not even praying.

And, of course, I felt guilty.

Our fast-paced, success-oriented culture has conditioned us to believe that times of non-production and rest are wasted time. That there is no value in literally doing nothing.

Have you bought into that lie as well? Is your datebook full on every single page? Do you have lists upon your lists? Do you feel like a failure if you haven't booked a coffee date or event with people most days of the week?

If my Lord—Jesus Christ, who had a pretty big assignment here on earth—felt the need to withdraw and seek a time of rest and solitude, then why should I be any different?

Today's verse came just after a time of intense ministry with so many people and responsibilities that Jesus and the disciples didn't even have time to eat! But after they withdrew for silence and restoration, God filled them up to pour out even more. What immediately followed was feeding the five thousand.

Are you weary of people and productivity? Give yourself grace-filled permission to relax and simply enjoy God's restorative gift of time alone doing nothing.

The crowds will wait. The kids will wait. The messy house will wait. But your soul will not wait.

Lord, You know how tired I am.
Give me courage to place all else aside
and rest in Your presence alone.

In order to remain healthy, our souls need solitude
with no agenda, no distractions, no noise.
Doing nothing does wonders for the soul.

JOHN ORTBERG

It's all in How You Look at It

How precious are your thoughts about me, O God.
They cannot be numbered!

PSALM 139:17 NLT

My great niece, waited with much anticipation as her second grade teacher announced the cast for their rendition of *Beauty and the Beast*. When her teacher came to my great niece, she smiled and said, "I think you'll make a perfect... Feather Duster."

Feather Duster?! That was not exactly what she had had in mind. She'd dreamed of playing the beautiful Belle in a yellow satin gown, but it wasn't to be. One of her friends was given that part, and she was happy for her. So, she learned her lines as Babette, the maid of the castle who is transformed into a feather duster, and helped put on a very entertaining play.

In February 2017 when Walt Disney Studios released the live-action version of *Beauty and the Beast*, my sister took her precious granddaughter to see it. As the movie was about to begin, she leaned over to my sister and whispered, "I was an *amazing* feather duster."

You see, she didn't remember that she wasn't chosen as Belle in her second grade play, rather she remembered that she was an *amazing* feather duster. It's all about our perspective, isn't it?

How's your perspective today? Or, to put it in different terms, do you see yourself as an *amazing* feather duster? God wants us to see ourselves as He sees us, and He thinks we're amazing because He created us. The Word says that His thoughts about us are precious and numerous! I want you to remember that the next time you face a disappointment in life. Meditate on how God sees you, and begin to see yourself in that same light.

Father, thank You for loving me like You do
and for always seeing the best in me.
Help me to see myself through Your eyes
and gain that God-confidence that
only comes through You.
In the mighty name of Jesus. Amen.

With Us in the Waiting

And now, O Lord, for what do I wait?
My hope is in you.

PSALM 39:7 ESV

Waiting is never fun. Waiting in line at the grocery store, waiting for our favorite ride at the fair, waiting for the tax refund check, waiting is rarely enjoyable. We have worked hard to shorten how long it takes to cook our food, register for college classes, even get our groceries so when we inevitably have to wait for something to happen in our lives, or wait for God's answer to our prayers, we tend to resist and grate against the delay.

Waiting is particularly hard when you find yourself completely out of options and at the end of your rope. My family has been there. We prayed desperately for rescue and waited, believing that God was going to answer our prayers for release from our burden and restore us to our former lives.

Except He didn't. Our rescue looked different than what we had prayed and longed for. Our answer didn't include being able to stay with lifelong friends and family in our comfy home on the coast of Florida. Our rescue was an eight-hour drive north to the northwest corner of

Mississippi, far away from those we loved. Our rescue came in the form of the biggest change we had ever endured and what became the biggest blessing in our future. At the time, I was grieved that God hadn't answered our prayers my way, but I have learned that He rarely does answer us the way we think He should. His answers are better.

Lord, I thank You again for not giving us
what we deserve or what we want sometimes.
Thank You for providing for us everything
that we need to grow and to mature
and to point others to You.

Blessed are the single-hearted, for they shall enjoy
much peace. If you refuse to be hurried and pressed,
if you stay your soul on God, nothing can keep you
from that clearness of spirit which is life and peace.
In that stillness you will know what His will is.

AMY CARMICHAEL

Keep Moving

Keep your heart with all vigilance,
for from it flow the springs of life.

PROVERBS 4:23 NRSV

My mother had a great sense of humor, especially about herself. That sharpened as she aged, and she was constantly giving me tidbits of wisdom about getting old. "Age may be just a number," she said, "but eighty-year-old knees have their own set of rules."

Mother picked out her own assisted living facility, and she insisted that my brother and I give her frequent driving tests. When I finally had to tell her I was more worried about her stamina and reaction time than her driving skills, she handed over the keys...and the car.

But while she gave up some privileges because of her age, she refused to give up exercising. She walked three miles a day until she was eighty-three. At eighty-six, she still did a mile around her facility—she even had a route mapped out. Every day at ten o'clock, she could be found in the common room for the daily exercises. When I asked her what kind of exercises they did, she grinned. "We're old people. We do old people exercises. We sit in chairs and move stuff."

And just as she believed in keeping her body moving, she kept her mind—and her faith—active. She studied her Bible daily, read novels, and did puzzles. Whenever I'd complain about something, she'd ask, "Have you talked to God about this? He's got more answers than I do."

She never let me forget that staying active with my faith would be my greatest asset, young or old.

Father God, may we always be active in Your love and light. Help us inspire others with our faithful words and deeds. Amen.

Our greatest weakness lies in giving up.
The most certain way to succeed is always
to try just one more time.

THOMAS A. EDISON

Metaphors of Praise

Your unfailing love, O Lord, is as vast as
the heavens; your faithfulness reaches beyond the clouds.
Your righteousness is like the mighty mountains, your justice
like the ocean depths. You care for people and animals alike,
O Lord. How precious is your unfailing love,
O God! All humanity finds shelter in the shadow
of your wings. You feed them from the abundance
of your own house, letting them drink from your river
of delights. For you are the fountain of life,
the light by which we see.

PSALM 36:5–9 NLT

There are times to allow the questions to fade, the struggle to disappear.

Like the apostle Paul in his letter to the Philippians, we focus on what is lovely, admirable, and noble (4:8).

When it comes to good, there is none better than our God.

The psalmist used metaphors above for God's attributes. Unfailing love as vast as the heavens. Righteousness like mighty mountains. Justice like ocean depth. He is Light. The Fountain of Life.

Soak it in.

Consider God's character and how it blesses you. How about creating a metaphor or two of your own? Does God's love envelop you like your favorite fuzzy blanket? Perhaps His presence is as refreshing as a warm shower. Is He like Your morning coffee: a sip of Him and life seems more doable?

Maybe He's as sweet as dark chocolate with raspberry swirls, bringing delight to your senses. Is He your Steady Eddy, the love you can always count upon?

His truth can be like the sun in a cloudless sky, blinding in its power. And His grace? It nourishes like a gentle, healing rain.

Oh what glory! Oh what delight!

God, Your attributes are beyond my ability
to describe, but I like thinking about
the wonder of You. I shift my thoughts to how
noble, lovely, and admirable You are.
You are all-glorious.

Always Remember...

Reflect on what I am saying, for the Lord will give you
insight into all this. Remember Jesus Christ,
raised from the dead, descended from David.

2 TIMOTHY 2:7–8 NIV

My friend confessed to me, "I'm so afraid that I will forget Jesus."

A young mother in her thirties, she was battling a brain tumor that was slowly removing her abilities and functions. And her memory.

Her greatest fear was that somehow the disease would progress to the point where she would forget knowing Jesus and being comforted by His love and promises. I assured her as best I could as we drove to her chemotherapy sessions. But I understood her concerns...

God was merciful and she continued to know the sweet presence of her Savior until she entered eternal rest a few months later.

Do you ever struggle with remembering? This seems to be a growing concern as we age. Even forgetting where we left our keys or glasses can send us into a tizzy. But nothing is more important than remembering Jesus.

In what was the apostle Paul's final letter, he urged Timothy to always remember Jesus. And His great love demonstrated in the crucifixion and resurrection.

Whatever is happening in your life today—even if it is so traumatic and earth-shattering that you would be tempted to forget everything you once held dear—please cling to Christ and the gospel story, the promise of eternal life.

Say His name aloud. Sing to Him. Remember. Jesus is here. Always.

Lord, even if I forget all else,
may I always remember You
and trust You in every situation.

When times get hard, remember Jesus.
When people don't listen, remember Jesus.
When death looms, when anger singes,
When shame weighs heavily, remember Jesus.

MAX LUCADO

Cheerfulness is among the most
laudable virtues. It gains you
the good will and friendship of others.
It blesses those who practice it
and those upon whom it is bestowed.

B. C. FORBES

Surprise, Surprise

*We know that all things work together for good
to them that love God, to them who are
the called according to his purpose.*

ROMANS 8:28 KJV

When my oldest daughter was diagnosed with pre-eclampsia at thirty-three weeks into her pregnancy with our first grandchild, I was surprised...and not in a good way. And, when her baby came via an emergency C-section after she'd been through thirty-four hours of labor—four weeks early—again, I was surprised...and not in a good way. And, when my adorable little grandson was whisked away to the NICU and I couldn't even hold him until he was three days old, again I was surprised...and not in a good way.

It wasn't the way any of us had pictured this pregnancy or birth. But knowing that the craziness surrounding such a blessed event hadn't taken God by surprise comforted us in the midst of the chaos that sometimes changed moment by moment. The end result—as bumpy as that road to recovery was for both my daughter and my sweet grandson—was a healthy, happy Mama Bear and Baby Bear.

Often our expectations of how things will go in life are not exactly, or even remotely, how they actually transpire. And, if your faith is easily shaken, that can really rock your world. Our family mantra throughout the ordeal was this: Though the attack is great, the testimony will be greater.

And it was and continues to be.

So if you're in the middle of some craziness in your life, wondering how you got there and why God is allowing it to happen in such a way, quit wondering and start proclaiming. Remind yourself that God isn't surprised by any of it, and He is still in control of all of it. Rest in that today, and remember that you're just working on an amazing testimony.

Father, help me to trust You during this unexpected craziness and rest in the fact that You're still on the throne. Amen.

Those who hope in [the Lord] will not be disappointed.

ISAIAH 49:23 NIV

It's Not about the Wallet

*For I am the LORD your God who
takes hold of your right hand and says to you,
Do not fear; I will help you.*

ISAIAH 41:13 NIV

Cara was worried. As a single mom, she had struggled to make her small salary cover all the expenses. Now her job might be over, and she had no idea what to do next. When she picked up her daughter from her church's daycare that afternoon, she explained that she would have to remove her child from the program.

The director sympathized. "I understand. But your daughter has made a huge impact on our other children. She's insistent on passing on what you've taught her about Jesus. Have you ever thought about doing that with more children? I'd love to have you on staff."

Stunned, Cara promised to pray about it. The money would be even less than she made at the other job, but she wouldn't have to cover daycare. After a night with God—and her budget—she accepted the director's offer.

All careers have ups and downs, and the "downs" can be tremendously difficult. But when we keep our focus on God—and what He wants us to achieve in our lives—we can maintain hope that He will see us through all circumstances, no matter how rough they get.

When we focus on working for Him and the impact His message can have on our world, our true calling in life will be made clear.

Lord, let us keep our eyes on You,
and not the world around us.
Show us Your way for our lives and how
we can impact others for Your kingdom. Amen.

Life is about making an impact,
not making an income.

KEVIN KRUSE

Hope Rekindled

Let us know; let us press on to know the Lord;
his going out is sure as the dawn; he will come to us as
the showers, as the spring rains that water the earth.

Hosea 6:3 ESV

When the world is in chaos, what a relief that our Lord is sure. When my life is upended by stress, financial difficulties, motherhood, and more, I can count on the Lord who made heaven and earth and can "press on" to know Him more.

I remember being completely parched in my spirit just a few years ago. We had completely started over just a few years before—a new state, new job, etc. We then found out our landlord had turned over his property to the bank and we were going to have to find a new place to live. The property we had been renting had been wonderful and I was horrified to learn we were going to have to leave it. We searched for nine months, every weekend, for a new place. I'm sure our realtor thought we would never find a new

---

Hope Rekindled

Let us know; let us press on to know the Lord;
his going out is sure as the dawn; he will come to us as
the showers, as the spring rains that water the earth.

Hosea 6:3 ESV

When the world is in chaos, what a relief that our Lord is sure. When my life is upended by stress, financial difficulties, motherhood, and more, I can count on the Lord who made heaven and earth and can "press on" to know Him more.

I remember being completely parched in my spirit just a few years ago. We had completely started over just a few years before—a new state, new job, etc. We then found out our landlord had turned over his property to the bank and we were going to have to find a new place to live. The property we had been renting had been wonderful and I was horrified to learn we were going to have to leave it. We searched for nine months, every weekend, for a new place. I'm sure our realtor thought we would never find a new home, and yet we *had* to; there was no option. I lived with much anxiety during that season. Change has always been difficult for me, but for some reason this one paralyzed me and I knew we could never find anything as nice as what we had. I grieved the loss even before it happened.

The end of that long story is that in God's timing and in His perfect plan He made available to us a home that I would not have ever dared to dream of and yet was prepared in advance for us as a balm to our drought.

Dear Lord, I thank You that we can know You and in You find hope. Thank You that the dry seasons are not forever and for the promise of spring and the rains to come.

Remember God's mighty deeds in your life.
Remember His kindness, His special tailor-made graces
that fell out of the sky like a gentle spring rain.

JONI EARECKSON TADA

Favor

I will give them a crown of beauty instead of ashes.
I will give them the oil of joy instead of sorrow,
and a spirit of praise instead of a spirit of no hope.

ISAIAH 61:3 NLV

Three little words: *I will give.* Not: *They will earn.* Gift, not wage.

What does God give? Beauty. Joy. Praise. And more! He bestows gifts upon His children as a king bestows a crown. Like a healer offers ointment.

Where once "no hope" resided, now lives a spirit of praise.

Isaiah 61 shows us Christ's mission. Jesus was sent to heal sad hearts, free captives, comfort the sorrowful, and give good news to poor people. He came to proclaim God's favor. The New Testament says He took us from a kingdom of darkness to a kingdom of light.

What is our part? To *receive.*

We are *favored.* Our new identity is the child of the King. The Lord no longer calls us servant, but friend. He tenderly takes off our shackles and anoints our wounds. He lifts our burdens.

Joy, healing, and freedom are ours. We grow in the experience and expression of these gifts over time, but they are placed within us the day Jesus transports us to the Light Kingdom.

Isaiah 61 ends with another "I will." This time the person speaking represents us. "I will have much joy in the Lord. My soul will have joy in my God, for He has clothed me with the clothes of His saving power" (verse 10).

Thank You, Jesus, for delivering me from
the spirit of "no hope" and giving me praise.
Thank You for comfort, healing, and freedom.
Thank You for lifting burdens.
I open wide my heart to receive Your joy.

I was delivered from the burden that had so heavily suppressed me. The spirit of mourning was taken from me, and I knew what it was to truly rejoice in God my Savior.

GEORGE WHITEFIELD

It's My Job to Love

*Dear friends, since God so loved us, we also ought
to love one another. No one has ever seen God;
but if we love one another, God lives in us
and his love is made complete in us.*

1 JOHN 4:11–12 NIV

Is it just me, or do people in general seem more judgmental and critical these days?

Perhaps it's because folks can now "hide" behind their words posted all over the Internet. They think anonymity offers license to be cruel, to mock or malign another person.

I understand the frustration of those who see a culture disintegrating and desperately need someone to blame. Helplessness makes cowards of us all, prompting the whole attack mode.

Have you been hurt recently by someone's words? There is plenty of hate to go around these days. But where is the plenty of *love*? You know, that which Christ-followers are called to share generously with everyone!

To love others is our duty in this fractured world. No matter what they say and do. We are to be Christ's hands, feet, and voice of love for the twenty-first century. If we don't, who will? Who is brave enough to go against the culture and extend compassion, welcome, and grace?

Frankly, I'm tired of trying to figure out who is on the right side and who is on the wrong side. How much better to trust God to sort out the judgment and consequences part. Wouldn't you rather err on the side of mercy?

Love others in the best way you can and leave the rest with Him. God is more than enough for our world today.

Father, will You help me reach out in kindness, compassion, and love, no matter what?

It's the Holy Spirit's job to convict, God's job to judge, and my job to love.

BILLY GRAHAM

Where's the Light?

When Jesus spoke again to the people, he said,
"I am the light of the world.
Whoever follows me will never walk in darkness,
but will have the light of life."

JOHN 8:12 NIV

Have you ever felt so discouraged in life that you just wanted to pull the covers over your head, eat some chocolate, and cry? We've all been there. On those days, people will often say things to offer comfort such as: "Into each life a little rain must fall," or "This, too, shall pass," or "There's a light at the end of the tunnel." All three statements are quite true, but when you're right smack-dab in the middle of a discouraging situation, it's hard to see that promised light at the end of the long tunnel. In fact, sometimes that tunnel seems so dark that you can't even find a faint glimmer of a light beam.

On those days, it's good to remember that Jesus is the Light! No matter how desperate your situation may seem, the Lord can deliver you out of it. No matter how hopeless you may feel, Jesus can restore your hope and your vision today. As you walk through the long tunnel, just know that you're not going it alone. Jesus is walking right beside you, and when people see you handling life's difficulties with such grace and peace, you'll have a lot of people following after you. Your light will shine bright before others, leading an illuminated path to our heavenly Father.

Father, help me to trust You more, and help me to remember that no darkness, no situation, no circumstance is too hard for You. I love You. Amen.

All the darkness in the world cannot extinguish the light of a single candle.

FRANCIS OF ASSISI

To Begin Again

The Lord will work out his plans for my life—
for your loving-kindness, Lord, continues forever.
Don't abandon me—for you made me.

PSALM 138:8 TLB

When I turned fifty-nine, I faced an uncertain future. I had no job and no savings or retirement to fall back on. I had great friends but no family where I lived. I spent a lot of time in prayer about the next steps for my life. Sadness and grief in such circumstances can easily overwhelm even the strongest believer. Hope can be a rare commodity.

But God is always full of surprises.

Just before I turned sixty, a job offer came out of the blue, but it meant moving to a different state and a new city. After even more prayer, I made the leap. All the details fell into place with unbelievable ease, leading me to an even deeper belief that this was the direction God wanted for my life. The job came with a number of challenges, which I eagerly embraced. It has been—without a doubt—the best move I've ever made.

No matter how dire our circumstances may be, God never gives up on us. He can guide and direct us, if we listen closely—and watch for those doors that fly open.

Father, help us to hear Your voice,
Your reassurance that You never abandon us.
You are always ready to provide,
whenever we rely on Your mercy
and blessings on us. Amen.

You are never too old to set another goal
or to dream a new dream.

C. S. Lewis

Do not remember the former things,
Nor consider the things of old.
Behold, I will do a new thing,
Now it shall spring forth;
Shall you not know it?
I will even make a road in the wilderness
And rivers in the desert.

Isaiah 43:18–19 nkjv

I am still determined to be cheerful and happy,

in whatever situation I may be;

for I have also learned from experience

that the greater part of our happiness

or misery depends upon our dispositions,

and not upon our circumstances.

MARTHA WASHINGTON

Finding Our Way Home

I have made the Lord GOD my refuge,
that I may tell of all your works.

PSALM 73:28 ESV

One of the darkest days of my youth didn't occur until my junior year of college while living at home. I'll never forget the day my parents met me at home to tell me the news that Mom had cancer.

After just a short while, I decided to head over to the school library to get some work done, and I found myself crying as I drove. In a few short minutes, I came face to face with a police officer in the middle of the road with his hand out telling me to pull over. Apparently I was speeding. In the midst of my sorrow, I had failed to look around me and observe, let alone look at my speedometer.

I wish I could tell you that the officer noticed my grief and let me off with a warning, but unfortunately he did not. There was no grace that day. Of course, this created more weeping and I turned around to head home because I was distraught over my very first speeding ticket.

After entering my home, my parents waited to find out if I was physically okay and then asked what had happened. Choking out the words, I shared how I'd been caught speeding. They laughed. I was horrified, but they were relieved! They thought I had been in an accident.

Needless to say, the laughter was necessary that day and my refuge of home was where I really needed to be in that moment.

Thank You, Father, that You desire for us to find our refuge and strength in You alone. I will be faithful to tell of Your works to those who follow.

But God is the God of the waves and the billows,
and they are still His when they come over us;
and again and again we have proved that
the overwhelming thing does not overwhelm.
Once more by His interposition deliverance came.
We were cast down, but not destroyed.

AMY CARMICHAEL

Delighted Trust

So cheer up! Take courage if you are depending on the Lord.

PSALM 31:24 TLB

Cheer up. Take courage.

The words can feel empty without the rest of the verse: if you are depending on the *Lord.* Now we have reason for cheer! Our God is the One who never fails. That doesn't mean life is without problems. It means no matter what life throws at us the Lord never leaves or forsakes us. He is always there, working in us and our situation, transforming both.

Remember who He is, this One we depend upon. He is Wonderful Counselor, Mighty God, Everlasting Father, and the Prince of Peace. He is also our Comforter, Provider, and Healer. He is the One who takes our burdens because He cares for us. He wipes our tears. He imparts joy and strength and hope. And in all of this He is still Abba—Daddy.

While His love is without the failings of human expression, while it is more powerful than that of any earthly father, He still relates to us with the joy, intimacy, and tenderness of a good Daddy. Imagine a young father tossing a small child in the air. What do you see? Smiles.

Confidence. Adoration. What do you hear? Squeals of delight!

What if our grown-up self tapped into the complete delight of child-like trust in our God?

Daddy God, help me live in delighted trust
with more happy squeals and less tears,
fully confident You will always catch me.
Help me to cheer up and live
with courage as I depend on You.

Cheer up ye saints of God,
There's nothing to worry about,
Nothing to make ye feel afraid,
Nothing to make you doubt.
Remember Jesus never fails,
So why not trust him and shout?

OLD SCOTTISH TUNE

An Unruly Tongue

A dishonest man spreads strife,
and a whisperer separates close friends.

PROVERBS 16:28 ESV

The rumor had been circulating for weeks, both around Mary's church and on social media. The tongues wagged, claiming Mary had embezzled money from the church's investment fund. The rumor also claimed Mary had been careful about covering her tracks, so her crime would be hard to prove. Or disprove.

Angry and hurt, Mary requested an audit and resigned as church treasurer. The audit cleared her of any wrongdoing, but the rumor persisted. Even more devastating, Mary tracked it to her best friend, who had made an offhand comment out of pure jealousy over Mary's position at the church. Her friend apologized, but the damage was done. Mary left the church, her faith in tatters.

One small comment. That's all it takes. Friendships—even careers—can be destroyed. It is human nature to share bad news, which is why Scripture speaks so strongly against it. As believers, we need to guard against the urge to spread ugliness about anyone, no matter how true we believe it to be.

And if you've been the victim of such foul gossip, please do not give in to doubt about God or lose hope in others. Their weakness is not your defeat. God stands strong with us, giving us the strength to face anything humans can dish out. We can rely on Him, take refuge in His Word, and forgive those who wound us. Our path is clear, and it will always lead back to the light of God's love.

Father, please give me the strength to forgive those who have wounded me. Show me a path of courage, and let me find strength in You and Your Word. Amen.

Let me be a little kinder,
Let me be a little blinder
To the faults of those about me;
Let me praise a little more.

ANONYMOUS

God Is Bigger

Peace I leave with you; my peace I give you.
I do not give to you as the world gives.
Do not let your hearts be troubled and do not be afraid.

JOHN 14:27 NIV

When my daughter was battling HELLP Syndrome as a result of preeclampsia following the birth of my grandson, I was so worried. As the doctor outlined the prognosis and discussed the risks associated with HELLP, I could physically feel fear fill the room. I immediately texted my prayer warriors to agree with me for Abby's healing, and I ended my text saying: "This is scary."

One of my sweet friends quickly texted back, "It is scary...but God is bigger than scary." As I read her words out loud to my daughter and her husband, we all agreed that God is bigger, and we began to proclaim that promise over every obstacle or setback. When her blood pressure skyrocketed to 190/103, we said, "God is bigger!" When the doctor ordered an EKG for fear something was wrong with her heart, we said, "God is bigger." And, when her blood levels tanked, requiring a blood transfusion, we again proclaimed, "God is bigger!" And He was! And He still is!

No matter what you're going through today, God is bigger. You can trust Him and rest in His promises. When He says He will never leave you or forsake you, He means it! When He says He can do all things, He can and will. God is bigger.

Thank You, God, that You are bigger than all of my problems.
Help me not to be afraid. I trust You, Lord.
Help me to trust You more. Amen.

Your problems may be big,
but our God is much bigger!
Your obstacles may be high,
but we serve the Most High God.

JOEL OSTEEN

Letting Go, Letting God

*Jesus Christ is the same yesterday
and today and forever.*

HEBREWS 13:8 NIV

Change is never easy, even when you are expecting it. School starts, and the house is suddenly quiet. We take a new job and suddenly have new coworkers we've never met. The pregnancy we've waited for finally happens. Even a good change can make for some anxious moments.

This can be especially true when the last child leaves home. Frantic preparations, long chats, and endless lessons on money, faith, and friends abruptly end. The house is not just quiet—it's empty. Anxious moments can cascade in: Did I teach her enough? Did he hear my warnings? Does she have enough money? Is he prepared for his classes? Will she pray and find trustworthy friends? Will he go to church?

What will I do now?

Trusting God's plan for our lives—for our children's lives—can be one of the hardest things we ever do. But we must remember that before they were our children, they were His. So were we. He loves us, guides us, and just as He never changes, neither does His plan for our lives.

Letting go is believing in His future for our lives. He will be with us every step of the way.

Father, we turn to You for comfort
and guidance as our lives work through
the changes You put before us.
Help us remember You planned our days
and that we can trust You to be faithful. Amen.

Prayer is the place of refuge for every worry,
a foundation for cheerfulness, a source of constant happiness,
a protection against sadness and depression of the soul.

JOHN CHRYSOSTOM

You Are Never Alone

My God, my God, why have you forsaken me?
Why are you so far from saving me,
so far from my cries of anguish?

PSALM 22:1 NIV

It can happen to anyone. We hit a low so low that we simply cannot climb out of the pit in our own strength. Worse, we lack the desire to do so.

I suspect this is exactly where King David was as he lamented in Psalm 22, wondering where God was as he suffered in anguish. Danger was all around, loved ones had betrayed him, and he felt absolutely deserted.

Many years later, God's own Son, Jesus Christ, quoted the same words as He hung on the cross, knowing God's plan but still feeling abandoned by His Father: "My God, my God, why have you forsaken me?" (Mark 15:34).

Are you disappointed in God? Then welcome to the company of sinners all, folks like you and me who authentically cry out to God in pain or betrayal. Go ahead and say those words to Him if you must. Guess what? God can take it.

Our God knows our hearts. He sees our pain and confusion. He realizes the consequences of our dangerous choices. And though He may not "rescue" us immediately, He does offer us a valuable gift here in the pit.

He gives Himself. He is here. No matter that you have yelled or even turned your back, God will never leave you. Your failures and falterings do not define you. You are defined as beloved.

Cry out. Then draw close. He is enough.

Lord, hear my cry, my wailing,
and come to me with compassion,
healing, and Your presence.

Throw at God your grief, your anger, your doubt,
your bitterness, your betrayal, your disappointment—
God can absorb them all.

PHILIP YANCEY

The Price of Pressure

For thus said the Lord God,
the Holy One of Israel, "In returning and rest you
shall be saved; in quietness
and in trust shall be your strength."

ISAIAH 30:15 ESV

It seems endless, doesn't it? That "to do" list for today or this week or this month? We say yes too often, promise others far too much, and never seem to give each task the time and effort it deserves. Mornings start before dawn, and work extends long past dusk. The treadmill of work isn't just about making more money. Sometimes it's just making enough to cover all the bills. But more often than that it's about feeling needed and knowing you've accomplished something valuable.

But there's a price. Exhaustion and stress change us. Our health deteriorates. Our tempers flare as our patience wears thin. This is a situation that can damage relationships, even the ones dearest to us.

So what do we do? We must find the word no in our vocabulary. Easier said than done...but it can be done. We may need to turn down valuable opportunities. Or refuse to add another activity to our children's week. But what's more important is to say "yes!" to time for God, for our families, and for rest.

Even God rested. It's one of His most vital gifts to us. To sit still and embrace Him and our loved ones. To give ourselves grace.

Lord, You gave us the miracle cure: rest.
Help us take time in each day to be with You
so that our spirit and mind can be
refreshed and renewed. Amen.

*Cheerfulness keeps up a kind of daylight in the mind,
and fills it with a steady and perpetual serenity.*

JOSEPH ADDISON

*And he said, "My presence will go with you,
and I will give you rest."*

EXODUS 33:14 ESV

God is glorified, not by our groans
but by our thanksgivings;
and all good thought and good action
claim a natural alliance with good cheer.

E. P. WHIPPLE

Joy Space

A cheerful heart brings a smile to your face;
a sad heart makes it hard to get through the day.

PROVERBS 15:13 MSG

A toddler's giggle. The fragrance of chocolate chip cookies baking. The glow of a warm campfire on a cool night. The dance of lightning bugs. The happy greeting of a golden retriever.

Joy is found in simple things. When life is hard, joy can seem elusive. But making space for joy to grow is not complicated. Does beauty lift your spirits? Plant a flower. Light a candle. Eat off a pretty plate. Opening yourself to joy doesn't have to be expensive or time-consuming. Often it's a decision to pause and focus—even for a moment—on something lovely.

Maybe music brings you joy. Crank up your favorite crooner as you tackle a task. Take three minutes to dance in your living room or to close your eyes and soak in a classical melody.

Nature can soothe a heart. You may not have the strength to climb a mountain, but a walk around the block in the fresh air cultivates joy. Rest beneath a leafy tree. Gaze at the night sky.

Being with good people fosters joy. So does listening to laughter. Google "babies laughing" or "great laughs" and take four minutes to fill your ears with the happy sound.

The decision to enjoy life's simple pleasures can seem insignificant when life's demands consume us, but making space for joy is a key for gaining the very strength we need.

Father, thank you for the little things that make life better. Please help me notice the things that bring good into my days, and teach me to make space for joy to grow.

Joy is strength.

MOTHER TERESA

A New Normal

Even though I walk through the darkest valley,
I will fear no evil, for you are with me;
your rod and your staff, they comfort me.

PSALM 23:4 NIV

It can happen unexpectedly, in the blink of an eye. Or it may come on slowly, like a progressive illness. Either way, your life changes forever, and whatever dreams of the future you had embraced are gone.

Such a life change can crush your soul and leave you devoid of hope. For a friend of mine, the diagnosis of a disease that would slowly destroy her physical and mental abilities left her drowning in her own sorrow. For me, the birth of a severely disabled child rendered me depressed and hopeless. A car crash left one of my prayer partners with chronic pain, which will be with her the rest of her life.

Pulling back to the surface after such an event can seem impossible. You can feel alone and—even worse—useless. No longer a "productive member" of society.

But you are neither alone nor useless. Psalm 23 is so familiar to believers that we may take the pure gravity of the words for granted. But we need to remember the absolute depths of despair that David suffered during his life. What gave him comfort, however, was the absolute reassurance that God never left him and would bring him comfort and hope.

We too can know that God is always by our side, and He will give us the strength to persevere and find hope in our "new normal."

Father, You surround us with Your love,
and we are grateful for Your strength.
Show us our new path, and help us
discover hope in what we still
have to do for You. Amen.

I am convinced that life is 10 percent what happens to me and 90 percent how I react to it.

CHARLES R. SWINDOLL

Only Light Drives Out the Darkness

You, Lord, are my lamp;
the Lord turns my darkness into light.

2 Samuel 22:29 niv

Do you ever jump ahead in the book you are reading to see how the story will end? In an especially suspenseful book, when it comes time to go to bed or leave to cook the family dinner, it can be difficult to walk away when we don't know how the story ends.

In seasons of difficulty in our Christian walk, it is easy to become discouraged. Our nature desires to know how it will end. If we know that all ends well, we can move on without fear or tears, but it is the unknown that evokes our emotions. The unknown makes us afraid. Many times our focus on the things that could go wrong hinders our actions and causes us undue stress and heartache. Our daily lives are no less different. As we walk through troubling circumstances, we wish to know in advance how our story ends.

The 2017 solar eclipse reminded us once again of the importance of light versus darkness. Our area was not covered in the totality of the path; we were at 94 percent. Yet so many people have remarked since then that they were shocked our area didn't get dark. What a wonderful reminder that light drives out darkness—even a mere 6 percent. The knowledge that God turns our darkness into light moves us forward with confidence, no matter what path we must walk.

He doesn't promise us that He will remove our difficulties, but He will be our lamp, and He will guide us through the darkness.

Thank You, Lord, for being our light in the darkness of our present circumstances, and I praise You for the knowledge that You will lead us through.

We Need Each Other

Friends love through all kinds of weather.

PROVERBS 17:17 MSG

As it sometimes happens in families, we were having some drama with our extended family, and it was really eating away at me. I felt betrayed, angry, hurt, and overall extremely disappointed in these particular blood relatives. I still loved them, but I definitely didn't like them too much during that season.

I needed to vent. I needed to cry. I needed a friend.

I had put on a happy face when I went to meet my sweet friend for dinner, but she could see I was hurting. She let me unload on her without any judgment, and then when I was finally through relaying the hurtful situation, I sighed and said, "I am so angry. I love them but I am just done."

She said, "I get it. I truly understand." And then she added, "You know, we choose our friends. We don't get to choose our families. Your friends—the ones you've chosen and the ones who have chosen you back—they can be even closer than family, and you have many of those."

She was right. I wiped my tears, gave her a hug, and drove home that night grateful for the friends God had placed in my life. Some were just for a season. Some live far away from me but distance doesn't separate our hearts; we're like sisters. And some are those forever friends that I can't imagine life without.

Friends, I've learned, are a different kind of family, but certainly the kind you treasure. If you're feeling lonely or sad today, reach out to a friend. Call up that friend you've been meaning to have coffee with and schedule a friend date. Take care of them because chances are, they've taken care of you on many occasions. Friends are a gift so be grateful.

Thank You, God, for friends. Help me to be a better friend to those amazing people You've placed in my life. Amen.

Walking with a friend in the dark is better than walking alone in the light.

HELEN KELLER

Just as You Are

For we are God's masterpiece.
He has created us anew in Christ Jesus,
so we can do the good things he planned for us long ago.

EPHESIANS 2:10 NLT

Oh, that comparison game! We begin it when we're still children. "I can't run as fast as she does." "He's smarter than me." "She's prettier." It continues into high school and adulthood. "I'll never get that promotion." "I won't look as good as she does in that dress." It even shows up in church. "He knows so much more about the Bible. I can't teach Sunday school with him in the room."

Stop. Thoughts like these are not humble, and they downplay everything God says in Scripture about us. "We are God's masterpiece." Let that sink in. You are a work of great art. God says so. And He has plans for you, for the work you will do for Him and for others. Each and every one of us matters.

We have a place in this world made especially for us. Comparisons with other people—what they look like or how much they've accomplished—are needless and distracting. Remember just to focus on who you are, and what you do will have an impact.

Just as you are. Right now. There is no one like you. And that's the best thing any of us can be.

Lord, help us remember that You created each and every one of us as individuals, perfect in Your eyes. You want from us only what You meant for us to be. Amen.

Act as if what you do makes a difference. It does.

WILLIAM JAMES

May the favor of the Lord our God rest on us;
establish the work of our hands for us—
yes, establish the work of our hands.

PSALM 90:17 NIV

Goals

Come to Me, all you who labor and are heavy laden,
and I will give you rest.

MATTHEW 11:28 NKJV

While visiting my grandson in the NICU, I studied the board hanging just left of his little incubator. The charge nurse had written WELCOME BABY and recorded his weight for the day and the names of his nurses for that afternoon. Then, my eyes scrolled down to a heading that read DAILY GOALS. Three actions were listed under it: TAKE BOTTLES. GROW. REST.

Over the next few days, I always checked my grandson's goals, and they were always the same. You know, those are pretty good daily goals for all of us. "Take bottles," meaning, eat. We have to eat to get physically stronger, but also we must eat of God's Word to get spiritually stronger. (It's interesting that in 1 Peter 2:2, the Scriptures are referred to as the pure milk of the Word.) Second, "Grow." We must grow up in all areas—physically, spiritually, and emotionally—if we are ever going to get out of that incubator stage of life. And third, "Rest." We have to rest our bodies and our spirits. Getting eight hours of sleep is almost unheard of in this crazy fast-paced world, but we still need it because sleep allows our bodies to repair, rejuvenate, and refresh. And, resting in God is equally important. Learning to rest in Him and in His promises instead of trying to figure out everything is not only a good idea; it's a God idea. (Read Psalm 23.)

So, I snapped a picture of the baby's daily goals and I keep it as a reminder on my iPhone, a reminder that I need to eat, grow, and rest so that I'll be strong, ready, and rested for that next adventure with God. Why don't you join me?

Father, help me to take care of myself,
both physically and spiritually,
so that I'll be strong, ready, and rested
to fulfill my calling in life. Amen.

Pray. Set Goals. Make a Plan. Work Hard.
Succeed. Thank God. Stay Humble.

ANONYMOUS

Saying Goodbye

Blessed are those who mourn,
for they will be comforted.

MATTHEW 5:4 NIV

Sooner or later, someone we love dies. Parents, grandparents, friends. It is a common, painful experience we all share. Sometimes death even seems to come in waves, one right after another. I lost my father and two friends in the same month. Twenty years later, I lost my mother and my daughter within fifteen months.

They were all hard, but I wasn't sure I'd ever recover from the last one. Even though my daughter's disabilities made an early death inevitable, an extremely wise woman once told me, "There's a huge difference in knowing it's going to happen and it actually happening. You can only prepare so much." She was right. I could put on a good face for friends, but grief consumed me. I spent months staring at the walls and wondering how I would go on.

But I did. God stayed by my side, lending me strength, directing me to people who could help, and offering that "still, small voice" (1 Kings 19:12) of comfort and guidance. And, as I healed, God opened doors to new opportunities that would allow me to find a new way of living without her.

Going on after the death of a loved one is never a gentle, well-lit path. It's a rocky journey through "the darkest valley." But God is there. And He will bring us through.

Lord, You stay by my side,
no matter how rough the journey.
Help me to lean on You, rely on You,
and trust You to guide me through. Amen.

A wounded heart will heal in time, and when it does,
the memory and love of our lost ones
is sealed inside to comfort us.

BRIAN JACQUES

May the God of peace be with you all.

ROMANS 15:33 ESV

A happy woman is one who has
no cares at all; a cheerful woman
is one who has cares, but doesn't let them
get her down. I can't be happy every day,
but I can be cheerful.

BEVERLY SILLS

# Joy, Not Grit

Be cheerful no matter what; pray all the time;
thank God no matter what happens. This is the way God
wants you who belong to Christ Jesus to live.

1 THESSALONIANS 5:16–18 MSG

Life can be serious business. The temptation is to put our nose to the grindstone—shut down desire, close off emotion, grit our teeth, and gut it out.

Exhausting.

Then Paul tells us to *always* rejoice. We add the weight of perceived failure to our difficult situation.

But what if Paul's admonition is less command than sage advice?

It's difficult to see life's blessings with head down, eyes focused on the tread of fatigued feet. The more we focus on the pain, the more it consumes us. So Paul encourages a different approach: cheerfulness.

How do we come to a place of rejoicing?

Recognize that God is there.

Send up bullet prayers—often! Notice what you're thankful for!

God is more tenacious than the biggest problem, and He *always* works for good. He completely accepts you, whether you're succeeding or failing in this present circumstance.

You are loved. Adored even.

He never forgets you.

What if we stop taking ourselves so seriously and let go of making sense of our circumstances? Instead we lift our focus from our worn-out efforts to gaze upon the One who never fails. With raised head we see the limitless sky instead of the finite ground. We notice the gifts, not just the struggle.

Joy and gratitude make our steps lighter.

Thank You God for always being with me and working in my circumstances. Change my focus so that I see limitless sky instead of finite ground, and empower me to live with a more cheerful heart.

Many people lose the small joys in the hope for the big happiness.

Pearl Buck

New Beginnings

Cast all your anxiety on him because he cares for you.

1 PETER 5:7 NIV

I had not planned to find a new church—I loved where I was. For more than twenty years, I had worshiped with them, sung in the choir, and eaten at all the potlucks. It was home. It was family.

It was now two hundred miles away. Not exactly an easy Sunday morning commute.

So I had been visiting churches in my new city, not quite believing how nervous I was to pull up and park in front of a new place. Questions overran my mind: Will I trip going through the door? Will this be my new "home"? What will the choir be like? Will I find a class or small group that welcomes me? Will I make a fool of myself?

Will God speak to my heart during worship?

Starting over at anything—a new church, a new job, a new school—can be scary and complicated. Being anxious is human nature. Stepping out of the comfort zone into the new takes a lot of prayer, courage, and openness to the "new" lying before us. Even when we know that God will be at our side, relying on Him can take more confidence than we feel at the moment that door opens and we walk through.

Lord, thank You for Your strength
and reassurance. I know You are there
no matter what new challenges
and experiences await. Amen.

To gather with God's people in united
adoration of the Father is as necessary
to the Christian life as prayer.

MARTIN LUTHER

The hour is coming, and is now here, when the true
worshipers will worship the Father in spirit and truth,
for the Father is seeking such people to worship him.

JOHN 4:23 ESV

Are You Brave Enough to Drink?

Everyone who drinks this water will be thirsty again,
but whoever drinks the water I give them will never thirst.
Indeed, the water I give them will become in them
a spring of water welling up to eternal life.

JOHN 4:13–14 NIV

Jill had never been so thirsty. Or so frightened. She watched the lion standing by the stream, thinking he was her biggest obstacle. But Aslan was there to offer her life-giving water.

For what do you thirst today? Perhaps you are ill and would give anything to feel better. Or you are desperate to find purpose in life. Maybe you are craving more hope, that God will intervene and make everything better.

Do you even *know* the source of your deep need?

Scientists say that often by the time we are finally aware of our physical thirst our bodies have already succumbed to dehydration.

Sadly, as we grow older, the ability to respond to thirst

is slowly blunted, rendering us numb to the very substance that will provide us life—water!

Today's culture offers many enticements for quenching thirst: entertainment, possessions, drug-of-choice, fast friends, and too-good-to-be-true business schemes. Have you grabbed such, only to find it disintegrating through your fingers?

God, our Creator and Redeemer, is the only One whose living water will never dry up.

Let's not be afraid if He first appears as a lion, looking like an obstacle to our happiness. And let's not wait too long.

Come to the waters....

Heavenly Father, I am finally willing to give up my desert experience and drink fully of You and all You offer me through Your Word. Pour out Your living water on my thirsty soul and bring me new life.

With Great Expectations

Commit to the LORD whatever you do,
and he will establish your plans.

PROVERBS 16:3 NIV

The Bride was excited but nervous. At the age of seventy-three, and after being a widow for twenty-one years, she was marrying again. She'd met her beau at church, although they'd been in the youth group together at the same church sixty years earlier. "It's like coming home," she said. Her friends teased her about the pitfalls of a new marriage, but she brushed them off. "We have hope and God. What more do we need?"

Even after a month, she still beamed. "God is all around us. He knows us. Why would He have opened these doors if He didn't want the best for us?" Her faith was contagious, and her friends rejoiced with her.

Ten years later, they were still delightfully happy. When asked their secret, she explained, "We committed the marriage to God and put our hope in His hands. Yes, there have been some troublesome times. Marriage is never easy, even for 'veterans' like us. But that hope never wavered. He brought us through."

This couple inspired everyone around them. Not by being blind to the trials of marriage—or the world—but by making sure they committed all their plans to the Lord. Her remarkable trust in God reminded her friends that when He is the priority, the rest of the details fall into place—or fall away. "Hope in Him," she explained, "is our finest treasure."

Father, You know us inside and out.
You love us unconditionally.
May we always give back our love
and trust. You deserve our best.

You study my traveling and resting.
You are thoroughly familiar with all my ways.
There isn't a word on my tongue, LORD,
that you don't already know completely.
You surround me—front and back.

PSALM 139:3–5 CEB

A God without Limitations

*A thousand years in your sight are like a day
that has just gone by, or like a watch in the night.*

PSALM 90:4 NIV

Being a caregiver is a full-time job. Not a forty-hour-week job, a full-time 24/7 job. Our family experienced caregiving when we raised livestock. We raised several sheep at a time for 4-H projects, and at one time a baby calf who needed bottle feeding, as well as a baby goat. We learned early on that these animals did not keep their eyes on a clock. When they were hungry, they were hungry, and when they needed help, they needed it right then. As their caretakers, if we didn't meet their needs, no one else would and so the responsibility was a grave one when they were babies, or during a sickness, or even when one mama gave birth—that was a long night!

Limited by the time we have, 24 hours in 7 days out of 365 days a year, the idea that God is not limited by time is awe inspiring! How in the world has God always been?

Before time, God was there. Before the earth was formed, God was there. After time has ended, and there is no more time, God will be there. One thousand years is like one day in God's sight. Astounding. We are limited by time and space, but our Creator God exists beyond those boundaries and the limits placed on us, His finite creatures. Of all the caretakers that we could have for our needs, isn't it amazing that the One who cares for our every need is limited by nothing?

Today, Lord, I just want to thank You for being such a great God over whom time and space have no control, but rather You control them.

How completely satisfying to turn from our limitations to a God who has none.

A. W. TOZER

One Touch of Nature

For I will satisfy the weary soul,
and every languishing soul I will replenish.

JEREMIAH 31:25 ESV

A study conducted in 2015 revealed that people are more productive and focused when they are exposed to the sounds of nature—babbling brooks, singing birds, whispering trees. But that study simply proved what anyone who's ever taken a walk in the woods or a stroll in the park already knew. Or anyone who's read the first book of the Bible, for that matter.

We are creatures of the garden. God put Adam and Eve in the midst of His astonishing creation and made them stewards over it. It is our legacy to feel at home in nature, to find woods, parks, streams, and trees refreshing and nourishing. Sitting on the patio with the morning coffee, listening to the birds and feeling a breeze against our skin can calm and renew us. Even listening to recorded sounds of nature in an air-conditioned room can stir our hearts and soothe our minds.

This is a gift from God we should not ignore. Just as He gave us work to do and a mission to spread His Word, He provided us with a longing for rest, a desire to remember and cherish His creation. What a blessing it is to settle in and allow it to nurture our souls.

Father God, You created us to walk in the garden beside You. Help us embrace and treasure all Your gifts to us, finding rest in Your embrace. Amen.

I lift up my eyes to the mountains—where does my help come from? My help comes from the LORD, the Maker of heaven and earth.

PSALM 121:1–2 NIV

An Attitude of Gratitude

Now, our God, we give you thanks,
and praise your glorious name.

1 CHRONICLES 29:13 NIV

Whenever I start feeling overwhelmed, aggravated, and a bit indignant, I'm quick to identify it in myself. During those seasons, I start using phrases like "I deserve better than that," or "I'm a nice person—this isn't fair," or "I always go the extra mile and no one appreciates me..." Yep, it's ugly. Just writing those statements makes me cringe. Just think what they do to the people around me who are forced to listen to my bellyaching? But, don't leave me hanging. I'm guessing you've also said similar ugly statements before.

You know how I get myself out of those seasons of ugliness? I immediately repent before God and start praising Him for the many blessings in my life. It's impossible to praise Him and complain at the same time. Developing an attitude of gratitude is key when trying to break the habit of the ugly "I" statements. ("I always go the extra mile." "I deserve better." And so on.)

Coupling your praise with action is also a great way to exit Ugliness Highway and merge onto Praise Parkway.

Take a few minutes each evening and write in your "Thankfulness Journal," recording even the smallest things to be thankful for that day. For instance, if you were able to find a front row parking spot at Wal-Mart, write it down. Another action you can take is writing at least one thank-you note each day. Send a card to a teacher who inspired you, or write a note of gratitude to your spouse for always being your rock. Adopt an attitude of gratitude and your season of ugliness will turn into an era of appreciation and peace. I promise.

Thank You, God, for the many blessings in my life. I am sorry for the times I am less than appreciative. Help me to maintain an attitude of gratitude, Lord. I love You. Amen.

God has two dwellings; one in heaven,
and the other in a meek and thankful heart.

Izaak Walton

The worship most acceptable to God comes from a thankful and cheerful heart.

PLUTARCH

All We Have to Give

Blessed be the God and Father of our Lord Jesus Christ,
the Father of mercies and God of all comfort,
who comforts us in all our affliction,
so that we may be able to comfort those who are
in any affliction, with the comfort with which
we ourselves are comforted by God.

2 CORINTHIANS 1:3–4 ESV

My mother had a saying that stuck with me from the time I was a kid: "If you're feeling sorry for yourself, go help someone else." She knew that all children could be self-centered, and I most definitely could. But Mother firmly believed focusing on the health and well-being of others made for the quickest cure for self-pity. And, as usual, she was right.

What Mother knew from experience—and Scripture spoke about two centuries ago scientific studies have proven to the world at large in this century: People who spend time volunteering, caring for family members, or supporting those in need are happier and less depressed. Lifting others up also strengthens the immune system and helps people avoid disease.

And this help doesn't have to be long term or complicated. Jesus, recognizing His disciples needed a break, suggested an afternoon of rest. Likewise, providing a needed ride to the grocery store or helping a friend with a school assignment can lift the spirit and provide a sense of accomplishment. Offering to stay with her children one afternoon can give a frantic mom exactly the break she needs.

As Paul wrote, God comforts us so that we can comfort others. Apparently, that is the true secret to happiness.

Lord, show us ways to give others the aid and comfort You have offered to us. Let us reflect Your love in all we do. Amen.

Then Jesus suggested, "Let's get away from the crowds for a while and rest." For so many people were coming and going that they scarcely had time to eat.

MARK 6:31 TLB

Our Strength, Shield, and Helper

*Praise be to the L*ORD*, for he has heard my cry*
*for mercy. The L*ORD *is my strength and my shield; my heart*
trusts in him, and he helps me. My heart leaps
for joy, and with my song I praise him.

PSALM 28:6–7 NIV

Whew! The pressure's off. It's not all on your shoulders.

No matter how difficult the day, the strength needed comes from God. You don't have to force or fabricate it because it doesn't originate from you. *He* is your strength. Those odds stacked against you? They're not too much for Him. He gives you the power to do what He puts in your heart to accomplish.

There's more good news!

Our Lord shields you. A shield protects, blocks, guards, and defends in battle. Like the offensive lineman who keeps the quarterback safe so he can do his job, our God blocks those things that would knock you backward. He defends you so you can move forward in what He's created you to do.

He *helps* you.

The world screams that we're on our own, but we're not. God goes before us, stands behind us, and surrounds us on either side. God knows exactly what we need even before we ask for it, and He is eager to empower us.

No matter the hiss of lie in our ears, the truth stands: God never abandons His people.

God is our faithful helper.

Your trust is well-placed.

I praise You, my God, my strength, my shield, my helper. My heart leaps with joy at the knowledge that You are giving me exactly what I need to move forward in every situation.

Never let the odds keep you from doing what you know in your heart you were meant to do.

H. JACKSON BROWN JR.

Overflowing with Joy despite Adversity

In all our affliction, I am overflowing with joy.
For even when we came into Macedonia, our bodies had
no rest, but we were afflicted at every turn—fighting without
and fear within. But God, who comforts the downcast,
comforted us by the coming of Titus.

2 CORINTHIANS 7:4–6 ESV

It's a paradox really. Overflowing with joy while in the midst of affliction. While many of us haven't been in mortal danger because of our faith like Paul experienced, we likely have experienced fighting without and fear within. We have felt afflicted at every turn—sickness, financial instability, sorrow, and grief. These life experiences don't come gradually or set apart from each other, rather many times we experience the overwhelming flow of one right after the other. So to read the words here "In all our affliction, I am overflowing with joy" grabs my attention.

The reason for his joy was because of the source of his comfort. God our Father, the one who comforts the downcast and diseased, the desperate and lonely, comforts us too. He sends reinforcements when we are bowed down with care and reminds us in His Word of all those He has cared for in times past. The words of David and Job, Abram and Ruth all mingle to mend our brokenness with the truth of His care and concern for us.

What comfort we can have as we rest in the everlasting Source of our joy! The examples of those who have gone before us fill us with confidence as we face whatever may come into our lives.

Thank You, Lord, for the written promises that ground us in Your truth when circumstances threaten. We praise You for the overflowing joy that can come only from You when life is hard.

Hope is the thing with feathers
That perches in the soul,
And sings the tune without the words,
And never stops at all.

EMILY DICKINSON

Will You Call upon God?

*Call to me and I will answer you and tell you great
and unsearchable things you do not know.*

JEREMIAH 33:3 NIV

Do you ever talk to God?

That conversation, my friend, is called prayer. Yes, even if you are asking Him "why?" Even if you have raised your voice in terror or pain.

God is listening to your words, but He is especially attuned to what's within your heart. Even if you don't know how to find the right words, He understands.

Because sometimes our feelings are simply too deep to articulate. Or we feel dry and distant, due to our lack of spiritual investment in God's Word and prayer. Maybe it's just too easy to follow the culture and try to do it on our own, self-sufficient to the end.

Whatever our struggle, how providential that in those times the third person of the Trinity—the Holy Spirit—intercedes for us.

Will you turn to your heavenly Father today, pouring out your heart in prayer? Prayers of praise for His constant presence, prayers of gratitude for His gracious provision, and prayers of entreaty for those you love who are suffering.

Our scriptural promise today is that if we do pray, His answers will be beyond our wildest hopes and desires. Perhaps that prompts some to call Jeremiah 33:3 "God's telephone number."

Will you call on Him right now?

Heavenly Father, please forgive my distance and my silence. When I don't know what to say, I often say nothing. I am here now and I thank You for Your patience and provision.

Don't measure the size of the mountain;
talk to the One who can move it.
Instead of carrying the world on your shoulders,
talk to the One who holds the universe on His.

MAX LUCADO

# Unfailing Hope

We know that suffering helps us to endure. And endurance builds character, which gives us a hope that will never disappoint us. All of this happens because God has given us the Holy Spirit, who fills our hearts with his love.

ROMANS 5:3–5 CEV

Ever feel hopeless?

Maybe struggle drains energy, and difficulties last years, not weeks. Paul says to rejoice in trials because through them we gain hope that doesn't disappoint us.

It sounds counterintuitive, but think about it. We tend to place hope in things of this world. Security comes from trust in our government or paycheck, confidence from health or success, happiness from human relationships.

Suffering shatters that kind of hope.

Jesus understood this when He said we would have trouble in this world. When He told His followers to be "of good cheer" it was because He knew where to place His hope—in His Father.

Jesus knew He would overcome because God would do what He promised. And He did, shattering the darkness by bringing us the light of a love that never fails.

When other hope is washed away through trial, we are established in *this* hope, the hope of an unending relationship with unfailing Love. Then we are "able to hold our heads high no matter what happens and know that all is well, for we know how dearly God loves us, and we feel this warm love everywhere within us because God has given us the Holy Spirit to fill our hearts with his love" (Romans 3:5, TLB).

Lord, establish my hope, steady and secure
in Your love. You keep Your promises,
shattering my darkness
and establishing me in light.

Hope is not simply a "wish" (I wish that such-and-such
would take place); rather, it is that which latches
on to the certainty of the promises of the future
that God has made.

R. C. SPROUL

Fresh Mercy on a Dreary Day

Yet this I call to mind and therefore I have hope:
Because of the LORD's great love we
are not consumed, for his compassions never fail.
They are new every morning; great is your faithfulness.

LAMENTATIONS 3:21–23 NIV

Someone once admitted, "The problem with life is that it's so *daily!*"

Do you agree?

Perhaps you are one for whom each day seems boringly the same as every other. Same routine of waking, working, and wearying. You feel lonely as four walls close in—a living space never visited by anyone.

For some it is hard to see beyond the mundaneness of daily tasks to the miracle gift of each new day.

And yet, who woke you up today? God. He has given you time in which to know His love, to sense His presence, and to believe His promises.

The prophet Jeremiah complained, "I am the man who has seen affliction" (Lamentations 3:1). He was just being honest. Life was hard and he was worn out and discouraged. But then he inserted this small little word—*yet*—and everything changed.

He remembered the Lord's great love, compassion, and faithfulness.

Friend, you are not alone in your grief, your pain, your loss. God knows. God cares. And He will bring you new mercies every single morning.

How will you get through another mundane day without despair? Call upon the Lord. Remember. And be grateful.

Lord, thank You for drawing near with fresh mercy, especially when I feel alone.

Everydayness is my problem.
It's easy to think about what you would do in wartime,
or if a hurricane blows through,
or if you bought that thing you really wanted.
It's a lot more difficult to figure out how you're
going to get through today without despair.

ROD DREHR

Heavenly Father,
Thank You for the opportunity to laugh.
Help me to find joy in everything that I do.
Let me laugh and be cheerful,
so that those around me will be blessed
by my smile and my optimism. Amen.

KIM BOYCE

Spring Is Coming!

As long as the earth remains, there will be
springtime and harvest, cold and heat,
winter and summer, day and night.

GENESIS 8:22 TLB

When snow lies long upon the ground, it can feel like spring will never come.

But it always does.

Talk to an elderly person about your trials and you're likely to be reminded that life has a way of changing. One day you have problems. After a time things work out.

The psalmists say, "Weeping may go on all night, but in the morning there is joy" (30:5), and "Those who sow tears shall reap joy" (126:5).

We all go through seasons when life hurts, but a rhythm is established on this earth. Sunshine and rain. Summer and winter. Weeping and joy. While it can *seem* like troubles never end, life has a way of changing.

The God of season is not stagnant, and He never forgets His own. "All who humble themselves before the Lord shall be given every blessing and shall have wonderful peace.... He cares for them when times are hard; even in famine, they will have enough.... Don't be impatient for the Lord to act! Keep traveling steadily along his path and in due season he will honor you with every blessing" (37:11, 19, 34).

Sweet friend, there is hope! With our marvelous God mercies are new every morning. Winter becomes spring. Darkness transforms to light. Tears turn into laughter.

Praise to You, Creator of seasons, for spring and light and laughter! I know You take care of me when my night cries grow long, and just as winter becomes spring, seasons of tears give way to seasons of joy!

You can cut all the flowers but you cannot keep spring from coming.

PABLO NERUDA

When God Speaks

*Trust GOD from the bottom of your heart; don't try
to figure out everything on your own. Listen for GOD's voice
in everything you do, everywhere you go;
he's the one who will keep you on track.*

PROVERBS 3:5–6 MSG

The hummingbird buzzed my head as I watched the sun rise. I didn't see it. Instead, I recognized the distinct whir of its wings. It was a hummingbird, there and gone, but unmistakable by the sound of its wings.

The hummingbird reminds me of the way I have learned to recognize the voice of my children. Each voice is unique and distinct. I remember the alert panic that enters your soul when you hear the cry of "Mom" with a note of something desperately wrong in it. I adore the joy of the sweet sound of laughter involving something fun and exciting. A parent just knows when it's their child and longs to meet their need.

This also reminds me of my heavenly Father! Just as I have learned as an ordinary person to listen to the sounds around me and connect them with what I see and know, how much more extraordinary is it that we can listen to what our heavenly Father says to us. How awesome it is that when we spend time reading His words, meditating on His Scriptures, and talking with Him in prayer, we can learn to hear the sound of His voice. The very fact that He knows me, and knows my name, and chooses to dwell in relationship with me fills me with awe!

Dear Lord, as I read Your Word, help me to listen and follow faithfully. Thank You for always being near, patiently and tenderly speaking through Your Word to me.

*Most elegantly finished in all parts, [the hummingbird]
is a miniature work of our Great Parent,
who seems to have formed it the smallest, and at the same
time the most beautiful of the winged species.*

J. Hector St. John de Crèvecoeur

Savoring Goodness

Open your mouth and taste, open your eyes and see—
how good God is. Blessed are you who run to him.

PSALM 34:8 MSG

Sweet, ripe blackberries. Decadent Belgium chocolate. The best flavor ever to touch your lips is not even close to the wonder of savoring God.

What about the most amazing thing you've seen? Maybe it's Orion through a telescope, the view from the top of a fourteener in Colorado, or a sunset on the California coast. No matter how awestruck you felt, it's nothing compared to gazing upon the Lord.

Isaiah reminds us of His wonder. "Who has scooped up the ocean in his two hands, or measured the sky between his thumb and little finger? Who has put all the earth's dirt in one of his baskets, weighed each mountain and hill?... Don't you understand the foundation of all things? God sits high above the round ball of earth. The people look like mere ants.... The rulers of the earth count for nothing....

Look at the night skies: Who do you think made all this? Who marches this army of stars out each night, counts them off, calls each by name—so magnificent! so powerful!—and never overlooks a single one" (40:12–26).

No one. Nothing. Compares with God.

Now wrap your heart around the truth: *This* God of grandeur offers Himself to *you*.

Wow, God! I am stunned by Your majesty
and overwhelmed by Your glory. I run to You
for all my soul longs for, knowing that
in tasting of Your goodness I am blessed.

Because the face of God is so lovely, my brothers and sisters,
so beautiful, once you have seen it, nothing else
can give you pleasure. It will give insatiable satisfaction
of which we will never tire. We shall always
be hungry and always have our fill.

St. Augustine

Do You Know His Voice?

He calls his own sheep by name and leads them out.
When he has brought out all his own,
he goes on ahead of them, and his sheep follow him
because they know his voice.

JOHN 10:3–4 NIV

My friend's computer knows her voice.

When her hands don't work properly due to rheumatoid arthritis, she speaks into the voice-activating dictation program on her computer and her words become blogs and letters and sometimes even books.

Would that I could be so immediately obedient!

When I discovered that this advanced technology can actually be trained to recognize one voice only, I was reminded of Jesus's words about how His sheep know His voice.

Can you recognize the voice of Jesus in your own life?

As you hear or read His words in the Bible, a devotional, or a sermon, do they penetrate your heart with a desire to respond? Sheep are animals who greatly need a leader and so they eventually build trust in their shepherd and literally do whatever he says.

I want to be as quick to respond to my Master, but sometimes I find it hard to discern God's whisper from all the many voices clamoring for my attention each day. You too?

The more time we spend with this Friend, the more familiar we will become with each different nuance of His commands. Will you take time to quiet your soul today and listen?

Dear Lord, I am finally quiet. And still.
Waiting to hear only Your voice.
Will You speak and then give me courage
to respond with obedience?

We must train ourselves in godliness so we can quickly and decisively recognize our Savior's voice. When He speaks, we move. When His Spirit nudges, we respond.

Joni Eareckson Tada

Glowing Faces

Those who look to him for help will be radiant with joy;
no shadow of shame will darken their faces.

Psalm 34:5 nlt

What do you see? Where are you looking?

That problem looms dark and ugly. Stare too long and your eyes glaze over. Your shoulders bend beneath the perceived weight. Your face becomes a thundercloud.

Oh my friend! Have You forgotten the One in charge? Do you remember His power, His faithfulness in the past?

Why not redirect Your gaze? He can handle what you cannot. He is capable, skilled at running the entire universe. He is also personal and prepared to manage the very thing that has you overwhelmed.

Did He not tell you to give Him all your burdens? There is no shame in admitting your need, no reason not to run to Him for help.

We move toward what we set our sight upon. Our eyes reflect what we see.

Lock your gaze upon the precious face of Jesus. See the radiant glory? Feel the love? Oh yes! Now you remember how tall and strong He stands in His God-muscle.

You're getting a face lift. Do you feel it?

Just looking toward the Lord eased the frown lines, erased the dark circles, softened the creases. The beauty of His countenance is reflected in yours. He smiles and your lips lift. His confidence boosts your own. The light that shines from His eyes is glistening in yours.

O Jesus! What joy it is to turn away from the problems and gaze instead upon Your God-muscles. I'm going to let You handle this one while I bask in Your radiance.

Adoration is the spontaneous yearning of the heart to worship, honor, magnify, and bless God. We ask nothing but to cherish Him. We seek nothing but His exaltation. We focus on nothing but His goodness.

RICHARD J. FOSTER

Every heart that has beat strong
and cheerfully has left a hopeful
impulse behind it in the world,
and bettered the tradition of mankind.

ROBERT LOUIS STEVENSON